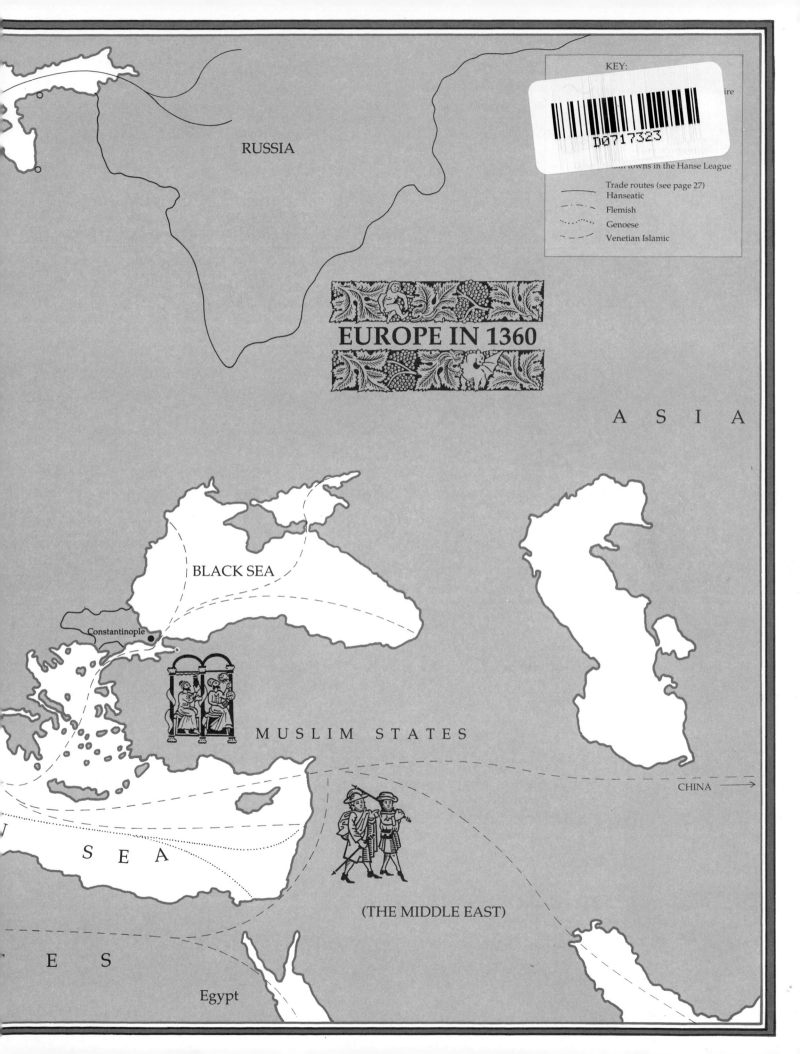

EUROPE IN 1360

RUSSIA

ASIA

KEY:

...ire

...ann towns in the Hanse League

Trade routes (see page 27)
Hanseatic
Flemish
Genoese
Venetian Islamic

BLACK SEA

Constantinople

MUSLIM STATES

S E A

CHINA →

(THE MIDDLE EAST)

Egypt

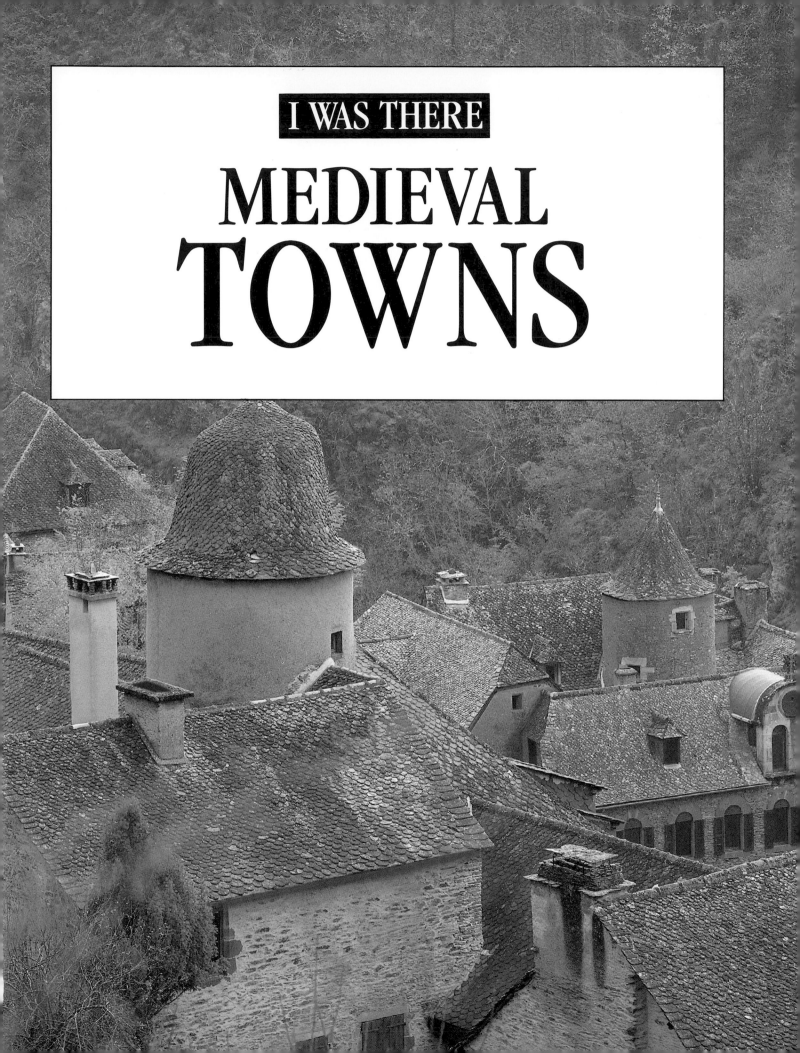

MEDIEVAL
TOWNS

I WAS THERE

MEDIEVAL
TOWNS

JOHN D. CLARE

Consultant Editor ANDREA HOPKINS

THE BODLEY HEAD
LONDON

First published in Great Britain in 1992
by The Bodley Head Children's Books,
an imprint of Random House UK Ltd
20 Vauxhall Bridge Road, London SW1V 2SA

Random House Australia Pty Ltd
20 Alfred Street, Sydney, NSW 2061, Australia

Random House New Zealand Ltd
18 Poland Road, Glenfield, Auckland 10, New Zealand

Random House South Africa Pty Ltd
PO Box 337, Bergvlei, South Africa

ISBN 0-370-31746-7

A CIP catalogue record for this book is available from the
British Library

Created and produced by Roxby Paintbox Co. Ltd
Aura House, 53 Oldridge Road, London, SW12 8PP

Directors of Photography Bror Lawrence, Tymn Lintell
Photography Charles Best
Second Unit Photography Bror Lawrence
Art Director Dalia Hartman
Production Manager Fiona Nicholson
Book Production Manager Avril Litchmore

Editor Gilly Abrahams
Series Editor Susan Elwes
Map/Time-line John Laing
Map/Time-line illustrations David Wire
Research Lesley Coleman
Typesetting Sue Estermann
Reproduction Columbia Offset Ltd, Trademasters Ltd
Printed in Hong Kong

ACKNOWLEDGEMENTS

Casting: Baba Rogers. Costume designer: Val Methering-
ham. Make-up: Pam Foster, Jane Jamieson, Emma Scott.
Props: Eleanor Coleman, Cluny South. Costume props
made by Angi Woodcock. Set design and building: Tom
Overton at UpSet. Photographer's assistant: Nicola Moyes.
Location manager: Martin Gee.

Roxby Paintbox would also like to thank the following:
Denny Edwards of Bermans International; Tim Angel
and Darren Fich of Morris Angel; Martin Blum; Lord and
Lady Saye of Sale, Broughton Castle; Cotswold Farm Park
Museum; Paul Conlon and Matthew Parkes of English
Heritage; The Dean and Chapter, Gloucester Cathedral;
Bert Griffin, D & D International; Film Wheels Ltd; Keely
Hire Ltd; Lavish Locations; Peter Breards, Leeds City
Museum; Martine and Michael Stewart, Wytham Abbey;
Jane Manning; S. J. Mitchell Transport; New College,
Oxford; Vardit Lunzer, Quintessa Art Collection; Nick
Redgrave; Joe Lintell; Rita and Lolita Catering; Roadrunner
Film Services; The Rector and Anne Hart of St Mary's
Church (Redemptorists), Clapham; The Dean and Chapter,
Salisbury Cathedral; Mrs Gascoigne of Stanton Harcourt
Farms; Tom Cooper at Young and Company's Brewery,
Wandsworth; Chris Zeuner and the staff at Weald and
Downland Open Air Museum; Trevor Wright.

Additional photographs: Scala, Florence p6; Reproduced
by courtesy of the Trustees of The British Library (The
Bridgeman Art Library) p6; Reproduced by courtesy of the
Trustees of the Victoria and Albert Museum, London (The
Bridgeman Art Library) p11; St Andrew's Church, Norwich,
Royal Commission on the Historical Monuments of
England p44; Archives Photographique Gerard et Adriana
Zimmermann, Geneva p45; Kupferstichkabinett Staatliche
Museen Preussischer Kulturbesitz, Berlin, photo Jorg P.
Anders p55; Reproduced by courtesy of the Trustees of the
British Museum (The Bridgeman Art Library) p62.
Illustration by David Wire pp44-5.

Contents

The Fourteenth Century

In the fifth century AD the Roman Empire was overrun by barbarian tribes such as the Goths, the Vandals and the Huns. In AD 476 the last Roman emperor was deposed. The Roman cities, with their impressive aqueducts and sewers, were destroyed or abandoned. Europe disintegrated into hundreds of small independent states.

Historians call the years between 476 and around 1500 the Middle Ages. During this time western Europe remained politically fragmented. Although there was a king of France, his kingdom was divided into a number of counties and duchies, each with its own ruler. Germany was ruled by the Holy Roman Emperor, but was split up into more than one thousand tiny states. Spain and Italy were similarly divided. Part of Spain was ruled by the Muslims. Central Italy was ruled from Rome by the Pope.

By 1300 many large towns such as Florence in Italy, Cologne in Germany, and Ghent in

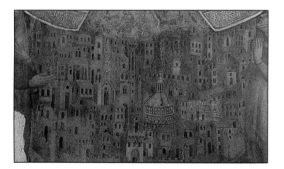

Flanders had gained control of the surrounding villages and had become states in their own right. In northern Europe a group of towns formed a powerful trading association called the Hanse League.

Feudal Society

Outside the towns, the basis of medieval society in western Europe was what historians call the feudal system. At the top of society were the lords, who gave land to the knights in return for military service. The knights rented tiny plots of land to the peasants, in return for their labour. Many peasants were the personal property of the knights. They had few rights and lived in appalling poverty and squalor.

A few women, such as St Brigitta of Sweden (who lectured the Pope about the corruption in the Church), were very influential in the Middle Ages. Men, however, dominated government and society, and even a kind man, such as Goodman of Paris, told his wife to 'copy the behaviour of a dog, which loves to obey its master; even if the master whips it, the dog follows, wagging its tail'. In public a woman was not supposed to laugh or cover her face unless she was ugly, and she was taught to look straight ahead as she walked.

According to the Roman Catholic Church, childbirth was the most important of a woman's tasks. It was also the most dangerous. Fully clothed and sitting upright on a birthing stool, the woman was helped by experienced midwives, whose unhygienic methods, however, often led to the death of the mother as well as the child.

Sickly children were baptized immediately, to prevent them from going to hell. Shortly after giving birth the mother herself went to be 'churched' in a ceremony conducted by a priest, because it was thought that childbirth had made her unclean.

Some sociologists claim that parents did not love their children very much in the Middle Ages. Yet they sang lullabies and rocked the cradle, and mourned when their children died – two out of every ten children never reached their first birthday.

Ignorance and Prejudice

The Muslim writer Usama ibn Muniqidh told the story of an Arab doctor who was asked to heal a knight with an abscess on his leg, and a woman with tuberculosis. He began to treat them, putting a dressing on the knight's leg and prescribing a refreshing diet for the woman. Suddenly a European doctor appeared. 'This man has no idea how to cure these people,' he said. Taking an axe, he cut off the leg of the knight, who died immediately. Then, declaring that the devil had got into the woman, he removed her brain and rubbed it with salt. She died instantly. 'I came away having learnt things about medicine that I never knew before,' the Arab doctor commented. Compared with their Muslim neighbours, the people of western Europe were uncivilized and ignorant, yet they continually waged war against the Muslims, whom they called 'infidels' because they did not believe in Christ.

Jews were welcomed by many rulers and town councils because they were allowed by their religion to lend money (the Church forbade Christians to become 'usurers'). They had, however, to live in separate walled areas within the towns to protect them from the townspeople, who unjustly accused them of drinking human blood, sacrificing Christian children and performing black magic. Foreign merchants were similarly feared and hated, and were frequently robbed, beaten up or murdered.

The Nature of Life

In medieval Europe, life was not cushioned by twentieth-century technology. There were few labour-saving devices, no washing machines or refrigerators, no cars or aeroplanes, no telephones or electricity, no painkillers or antibiotics. Everything had to be made laboriously by hand, and was therefore relatively more expensive – a pair of leather boots, for example, cost a ploughman two months' wages.

Poverty and brutal crime were commonplace in everyday life. Town records are full of stories such as that of William de Grymesby, a London shopkeeper. At midnight one Tuesday in January 1322, he beat to death Reginald de Freestone, an arrow-maker whose singing and shouting had kept him awake. De Grymesby was arrested and his personal possessions confiscated. They comprised two small pigs, a broken chest and table, one pair of worn linen sheets, a blanket and a linen cloth.

In many European countries torture was an accepted part of questioning by the authorities. Punishments were harsh, immediate and public. When Sir Gilbert Middleton was found guilty of ambushing and robbing the Bishop of Durham in 1317, he was dragged through the streets to the gallows, hanged, taken down alive and beheaded. His head was sent to London and his heart was burned at the gallows. His body was quartered and the four parts sent to Newcastle, York, Bristol and Devon, to be displayed as a warning to others.

During the fourteenth century, civilization in western Europe seemed to go backwards. There was continual warfare – notably the Hundred Years War (1337-1453) between England and France. Wandering bands of soldiers looted and pillaged the countryside. In the middle of the century a plague called the Black Death carried off a third of the population. 'People said and believed "This is the end of the world"', an Italian chronicler wrote.

Far left: a fresco of Florence, painted in 1352. Above left: a scene from the Luttrell Psalter (see page 62).

Farming and Famine

Only a tiny proportion of the population of medieval Europe lived in the towns. Most people lived in the country and worked on the land. Towns depended on the local peasant farmers to provide them with food.

Farming technology was simple. Ploughs were pulled by oxen; sowing was done by hand. Each year, part of the land was left fallow (uncultivated) to recover its fertility.

During the early Middle Ages the population had grown steadily, stretching food supplies to the limit. Towards the end of the thirteenth century, however, the weather became wetter and colder (some historians call this period the Little Ice Age). The crops failed. In addition, between 1316 and 1325, murrain (disease) killed large numbers of cattle and sheep. In some years the lack of sun meant that sea water could not be

evaporated to produce salt, which was needed to preserve meat.

Although people could add rabbits, wild birds and berries to their diet, Europe suffered more than 25 years of famine in the century after 1272. Many people starved. According to one chronicler, in 1315 hungry people ate dogs, cats, the dung of doves – even their own children – to stay alive.

Theft and robbery increased. Almsgiving (charity) decreased. Habitually underfed, people – particularly the old and very young – lost their resistance to diseases such as typhoid, dysentery and influenza. The Black Death was not the only natural disaster in the fourteenth century; it was the culmination of many years of disaster.

The peasant and his family work from dawn to dusk in miserable conditions. The oxen are difficult to manoeuvre and the primitive plough cuts only a shallow furrow.

The Medieval Town

Towns developed in the Middle Ages for a number of reasons. Some grew up around an important monastery or castle, where people hoped to be safe from attack. Large villages, where local farmers gathered to sell their produce, developed into market towns. A trading centre – a harbour, the confluence of two rivers or a busy crossroads – often became the site of a growing town. Faced with hardship and oppression on the land, many peasants ran away to live in the towns. If they managed to avoid capture for a year, they became free men.

These growing towns were situated on land held by the local lord. The townspeople had to pay him feudal dues and work on his land just like the local villagers. An important event in the development of a town, therefore, was the granting of a charter by the king or a local nobleman, whereby the town became a borough. Its leading citizens – the burgers – were released from the lord's control and became 'freemen' of the city. The charter gave them the right to hold a market, to elect a mayor and a town council, make their own laws and administer their own justice.

The rich burgers lived in houses built of stone, to reduce the danger of fire. Less wealthy merchants built timbered houses

made from a wooden frame packed with mud, dung and horsehair. As building land was expensive, they built upwards. Building plots were long and thin and many had an alley down the side of the house for access to the warehouse and stables.

Strong walls round the edge of the town help to keep out invading armies. The market-place, church and administrative buildings are in the town centre.

Right: many nobles have town houses to which they often go, passing into the city through the strongly fortified gatehouse. The poor live in hovels near the town walls. There are few public facilities, so they have to do their washing in the river.

A Medieval Street

Medieval towns were surprisingly small. Few had more than two thousand inhabitants. Even the largest towns, such as Florence and Paris, had populations of less than two hundred thousand.

Nevertheless, hemmed in within their walls, towns were crowded and noisy places. Carts and horses clattered down narrow, cobbled streets. Town criers shouted out details of fairs, houses for sale and forth-coming marriages. Beggars cried out for alms. Pedlars and shopkeepers called out their wares – 'Pepper and saffron', 'Ribs of beef and many a pie!' Bells rang continually, announcing the opening of the town gates, the start of market trading, church services, council meetings – even the birth of a royal princess. In Florence a work bell marked the start and the end of the working day.

Although town councils paid 'scavengers' to clean away refuse, there were frequent complaints about the state of the streets. People threw their rubbish and excrement into the street or river. In 1365 Lincoln in the north of England smelt so bad that foreign merchants refused to visit the town until it had been cleaned. People who could not afford to buy fresh water (brought in from outside the town by the water-sellers) had to take it from the public fountains, from a well in their back yard – or from the river.

At night, the dark, unlit streets were the haunt of thieves. In some places the town council organized a rota of citizens who formed a 'watch' (an amateur police force), but most towns simply closed the gates at dusk and rang a curfew bell. Law-abiding citizens closed the window shutters, barred the door and stayed inside.

In the street are a pedlar, a pieman, a water-seller, a crippled beggar, a farmer taking his horse to market and, next to the draper's shop, a knife-grinder.

Inside a Merchant's House

The ground floor of a merchant's house was often rented to a craftsman. On the first floor there was the main hall, where the family ate and entertained guests. On the floor above there were the other family rooms, including the solar (for activities such as embroidery and reading), a parlour (for private conversations and business meetings) and the bedrooms. Very rich households had a small chapel and employed a chaplain. The servants' quarters were in the attic.

Although houses did not have bathrooms or running water, medieval people were not permanently filthy. Most towns had public bathhouses (Paris had 26 in 1292) and some people bathed twice a day. Books on household management advised ladies how to organize the cleaning of their houses. A wife was also expected to supervise the candlemaking, sewing and brewing, and to help with her husband's business.

Below: the merchant is more comfortable in his solar than the nobleman in his castle. His wife cards wool with two brushes, disentangling the strands so that they can be spun on the spinning wheel beside her. The household valuables are locked in the cupboard. A carpet, too expensive to walk on, hangs on the wall.

Left: the merchant's chair has a high back and sides, to protect him from draughts; the window openings have no glass, only wooden shutters.

The merchant's children often play with a whip and top (far left), or with the bleached knucklebones of sheep (centre), which they toss in the air, trying to scoop up a bone from the floor before catching the falling bones.

In the Kitchen

In 1315 the household accounts of Lord Lancaster, a wealthy English nobleman, came to £7,958. He spent £1,000 on clothes; 4,100 candles cost him £32 and a lost horse £8. However, £3,751 – nearly half the budget – was spent on stocking the buttery (storeroom for food and wine) and the kitchen. This shows how important food was to the rich.

A cook was a respected person and was well paid. Both men and women became cooks. They were expected to bake the bread, cook the meals and lay the tables. Obtaining provisions occupied much of their time. Nicholas Litlington, Abbot of Westminster in the fourteenth century, employed a cook named Walter on his estate near Oxford. In Holy Week, 1372, finding he had no fresh salmon, Walter rode 70 miles (113 kilometres) to London to buy two river salmon.

Except for locally available produce such as apples and cherries, medieval cooks had

to use dried fruit – currants, prunes and dates. In the households of the nobility, few vegetables apart from onions were used, because they were considered to be the food of poor people. Instead, cooks served a vast range of meats including magpie, squirrel, antelope, cormorant, porpoise, whale, seal and swans' brains. Hedgehogs, advised a French recipe book of 1393, should be skinned, cleaned and roasted like chicken.

Cooks created exotic dishes using herbs, spices and strongly flavoured sauces – in part to disguise the taste of the meat, which had been preserved in salt and was often starting to go bad. An English recipe for 'German broth' instructed the cook to boil diced rabbit with almond milk, cypress root, ginger, rice flour, sugar and bugloss (a wild flower).

In many merchants' households in the towns, the kitchen is in a separate building; the oven and the fire – where meat is roasted on a spit – are a fire risk. The kitchen is a centre of activity, especially in winter when it is the warmest room in the house.

The Power of the Church

Most people in medieval Europe were very religious. They took their babies to church to be baptized and their dead were buried in the churchyard. They prayed to the saints – for example, to St Anthony to help them find lost objects, and to St Nicholas (Santa Claus) to protect their children. Most towns had a patron saint.

Frightened of annoying God in this life, people were terrified of going to hell in the next. Nobles and rich merchants left money for priests to say Masses for them when they died. They believed that after death – even if they managed to avoid hell – they would have to spend thousands of years in purgatory, to be cleansed of their sins. When Pope Boniface VIII declared 1300 a jubilee year, two million pilgrims flocked to Rome, hoping to reduce their time in purgatory.

Monks and Nuns

In the Middle Ages a wealthy family would often send a daughter to a convent or a younger son to a monastery. Monks and nuns were supposed to live by the threefold rule of prayer, work and study: they had to attend six church services a day and spend the rest of their time working in the fields and reading the Bible. They vowed to live in poverty, to obey the abbot or abbess and to remain unmarried all their lives.

During the thirteenth century, as towns grew more important, the orders of Franciscan and Dominican friars were founded. They did not shut themselves away in monasteries, but lived amongst the townspeople, distributing alms, tending the sick and preaching the gospel. Sometimes a friar would cause a riot when, accompanied by a mob of townspeople, he went into the Jewish quarter to try to convert the Jews to Christianity.

Church and State

The Church provided many essential services. Abbots and bishops acted as advisers to the rulers. Clerics were used by the government and the nobility to write letters and to keep records. In an age before the printing press, monks copied all the books by hand.

In the monasteries, local invalids were cared for by a monk called the infirmarer, the poor were given charity by the almoner and travellers were looked after by the hospitaller. To pay for these services, kings and nobles gave land and money to the Church. In

addition, the Church took a tithe (tenth) of the peasants' produce and a tenth of the merchants' profits.

As a result the Church was both rich and influential. Bishops rode to war like princes, with large armies raised from their estates. Anyone who was suspected of disagreeing with the Church's teaching was called a heretic and burned at the stake. In 1302 Pope Boniface issued the bull (papal law) *Unam Sanctum*, which stated that the pope had complete authority not only over the Church but over all kings and rulers. The bull declared that obedience to the pope's wishes was necessary for salvation – those who disobeyed would not go to heaven.

Yet one year later King Philip IV of France captured and imprisoned the 86-year-old pope, who died of shock. The next pope, Clement V, was a Frenchman. Instead of living in Rome like all the previous popes, he settled in Avignon, a city in Provence. For the next 70 years all the popes were French and lived in Avignon.

Pope Gregory XI returned to Rome in 1378, but after his death a schism (split) occurred amongst the cardinals (the leading churchmen). Some supported the Italian candidate, Urban VI; others elected Clement VII and moved back to Avignon. The 'Antipope', Clement VII, was lame and had a squint; he was violent and merciless. Urban became crazed with power. Until the end of the fifteenth century there were two popes, each of whom excommunicated the followers of the other. 'These are things to crush one's faith,' wrote an Italian chronicler.

Monks pay more attention to cleanliness than most people. They wash in the *lavatorium* (above left), from which comes the word lavatory. Left: when a young boy joins a monastery, he is given a monk's tonsure (haircut). Right: some friars try to keep their vows of poverty. They distribute alms to the poor, while they themselves live by begging; wealthy townspeople often try to avoid them.

Corruption in the Church

The cathedral's central position in the town, its size, expensive decoration and stained glass, were a reflection of the wealth and power of the Church.

The priest led the worship in Latin, from behind a wooden rood screen. Most people, therefore, found the services dull and meaningless. The congregation gossiped, squabbled and even fought while the service was in progress. At Exeter Cathedral, bored choirboys dropped hot candle wax onto the heads of those seated below them.

To ordinary people the Church seemed full of corruption. At Bury monastery in England, 80 monks had 111 servants working for them. A family in mourning would be pestered by priests and friars wanting to conduct the burial – and receive the fees. Even the Pope sold dispensations (the right to commit a sin), indulgences (to reduce the time spent in purgatory) and benefices (positions in the Church). Pope John XXII was so wealthy that he paid 1,276 gold florins for 40 pieces of fine cloth. 'Spirituals' (a group of Franciscan monks who insisted on obeying their vow of poverty) were accused of heresy, thrown into dungeons and tortured!

In 1340 the Pope's adviser, who had investigated the monasteries, listed 42 complaints against monks, including having affairs with nuns, plotting to murder the abbot and refusing to sleep in their clothes. Because of these things, many people hated the Church. In 1347 the people of Gaeta in Italy seized a papal tax-collector, stripped and imprisoned him, and confiscated the tax money.

By the fourteenth century most of the great European cathedrals are almost finished. The high walls (left) have been built by masons using simple tools, wooden scaffolding and wheel-pulleys (below).

Bottom: Salisbury Cathedral clock. Because the clergy need to know when to begin the services, the Church is one of the first institutions to use clocks.

Inside, the cathedral is richly decorated (right). The services are long rituals, meant to be a mystery (wonder) to ordinary people.

Holy Day Parade

Medieval people believed in miracles. Their faith stopped them despairing at the disease, war and famine around them. They went on pilgrimages to holy shrines and collected relics – holy objects, such as the fragment of a saint's bone – which they thought would have the power to help and heal them. In 1346 a church at St Omer in France claimed to possess a lock of the Virgin Mary's hair, a piece of Jesus' cradle and a piece of stone on which were carved the Ten Commandments.

Dozens of saints' days were celebrated as religious festivals. The University of Paris observed 102 saints' days a year, and the city of Florence had over 120 holy days, although people did not use them for worship as they were supposed to do. 'They spend little time in hearing the Mass, but in games, or in taverns, and in arguments at the church-doors,' complained a fourteenth-century writer. On holy days (and also on Sundays) the lower classes took a rest from work, from which comes the modern word holiday. At certain festivals 'the world was turned upside-down'; workmen ruled their masters, and pupils commanded their teachers.

A market was often held on a holy day, and travelling merchants, pedlars and tinkers mingled with the townsfolk, bringing the latest news from other towns. For entertainment, there was wrestling, dancing, football, archery, cock-fighting and bear-baiting (dogs attacking a chained bear). The Church criticized these things, especially 'the way of dancing, which leadeth to hell', as the Italian poet Petrarch described it.

On the feast of St James, a fragment of one of the saint's bones is paraded through the town in a silver reliquary, while the people enjoy the holy day and watch the performers.

Mystery and Miracle Plays

As most medieval people could not read, priests had to find other ways to teach them. Churches were decorated with stained glass, paintings and carvings depicting biblical events and stories of the saints. Early in the Middle Ages, priests began to act short mimes, which later became mystery plays (about the life of Christ) and miracle plays (based on the stories of the Bible and the early Church). The people of Paris held a cycle of plays lasting four days; the London cycle lasted a week.

The characters were played by local craftsmen. *Noah's Ark*, for example, was acted by the shipwrights; the fishmongers performed *Jonah and the Whale*. In France the actors were organized into *confréries pieuses* (holy brotherhoods).

Actors often spoke from carts (called mansions) which were pulled round the streets. There were costumes, special effects and scenery. Weights and pulleys raised Jesus from the tomb. A play called *Le Jeu d'Adam* (Adam's Play) required silk curtains, fragrant flowers and fruit for the Garden of Eden. Another, performed before the Holy Roman Emperor in 1378, featured a crusader's ship. During a play common in both England and France, devils – wearing wolfskins, sheep's heads and bulls' horns – ran about throwing fireworks to frighten the audience.

The plays were crude and bloody. A local curate playing Jesus almost died on the cross and a Judas who hanged himself too enthusiastically was revived with difficulty. The spectators roared with laughter when the actors who played the Virgin's donkey dropped fake manure or hee-hawed at inconvenient moments.

God, wearing a gold mask, a wig and a beard, cannot stop the devil claiming a sinner. Preachers hope that such scenes will convert people to a better life.

Craftsmen and Merchants

In a typical town, up to half the adult male population would be craftsmen. People of the same trade often lived close together; in many towns, modern street names such as Cutler Street, Silver Street and Tanners Lane (tanners were leather workers) recall the occupations of the people who lived there in the Middle Ages. In York, in the north of England, all the butchers lived and worked in a street still called The Shambles (the name given to the butchers' tables). These groups of craftsmen and tradesmen often organized themselves into associations called guilds (see page 28).

In most towns, markets were held two or three times a week. The townspeople bought grain, livestock, firewood, eggs and milk from the local farmers. They erected stalls and sold bread, ale, candles, pottery, shoes, knives and clothes. Only the rich had ovens; the less wealthy had to take their dough to be cooked by a baker, who also cooked their Sunday dinner.

Everything was sold in bulk – grain by the bushel (36 litres), butter by the gallon (4½ litres), firewood by the hundredweight (50 kilograms). Cheeses were sold whole, whatever their size. Apart from barrels, there were no containers or wrappings, although butter was wrapped in the leaves of the butterbur plant.

The guilds usually had strict rules about where, when, and for how long people could trade – it was an offence, for example, to trade before the market bell had rung. Each town had regular assizes (meetings of officials who fixed weights, measures and prices, especially of bread and ale). There were many other small, seemingly silly, rules; in London, for instance, fishmongers could only sell fish that was more than three days old, so that the fishermen could try to sell it first.

Most towns also had a market court,

nicknamed the piepowder court after the traders who sat in judgement there (the French phrase *pieds poudres* means dusty feet). Punishments were usually made to fit the crime. Water-stealers might have to walk through the town with leaking buckets on their heads; a trader who sold bad wine would have to drink his own brew in public – the rest was poured over his head.

Traders and Fairs

The greatest trade of the Middle Ages was in cloth – finely-woven Flemish cloth was a luxury item, and the towns of northern Italy produced silk, velvet and brocade interwoven with threads of gold and silver. Italian merchants developed trade links across the whole of Europe. During the Hundred Years War they stopped travelling by packhorse through France, and went instead by ship through the Strait of Gibraltar direct to the ports of the north, such as London, Ghent and the Hanse towns.

Merchants also traded many other goods throughout Europe and the Middle East. They formed partnerships by signing a *commenda* – an agreement whereby one of them would put up the money, while the other would undertake the dangerous journeys to foreign lands. They would then share the profits.

Instead of carrying large sums of money, traders used bills of exchange (a type of international cheque). Important banks grew up, especially in Italy, and Italian bankers became as unpopular as the Jewish money lenders.

Most of this international trade was done at the great fairs, which took place only once or twice a year and lasted up to a fortnight. The fairs held in Champagne, a province of eastern France, were famous throughout Europe, and the King of France himself ensured that merchants could cross his country in safety. Rich families sent their stewards to the fairs, to buy provisions for the winter and to obtain articles not available locally – from honey and beeswax to Hanse amber and fine porcelain from the East.

Merchants and some of their wares. Opposite page, below left: the English merchants sell coal, cloth, corn, wool and metalwork. Opposite page, below right: Italian merchants trade in luxury goods such as jewellery, glassware, embroidered brocade, silk, jewelled hats and armour. Above left: from the East come jewels, silk, carpets and 'spices' – everything from flavourings (such as ginger, cinnamon, cloves and nutmeg) to medicinal plants and herbs. Above right: the Hanse merchants trade in Scandinavian tar, furs, rope, salt, goose feathers and amber jewellery.

Opposite page, above: because so few people can read in the fourteenth century, shop signs show what goods or services are available.

Guilds

Only guild members were allowed to trade in the city. They could not work at night or under-charge. By these methods the guild kept production down and prices up. Members who failed to maintain high standards of workman-ship were fined or expelled from their guild.

Women rarely became full guild members. Some guilds (for instance the barbers and the dyers) accepted women, and widows were allowed to practise their husbands' trades, but most guilds tried to exclude them altogether. Women, nevertheless, worked as butchers, ironmongers, shoemakers, hot-food sellers, bookbinders, embroiderers and goldsmiths. Domestic activities such as silkmaking, spinning and brewing were exclusively female occupations.

Many guilds provided a welfare system. The Guild of Mercers (dealers in cloth) in London charged 6d. a week (see page 63) and used the money to help poor members. Wealthy guilds started schools, ran retirement homes, paid for the funerals of poor guild members and arranged entertainments on holy days.

In some towns leading merchants formed an association called a merchant guild. The guild had a royal charter and took charge of the government of the town.

Wealthy people go to the tailor's to buy fine clothes and hats. They spend their money on things like food and clothing which give them immediate pleasure, rather than on longer-lasting goods such as furniture.

Below: buttons, introduced from the Middle East, are a novelty in the fourteenth century. Sometimes they are made of gold, silver or bone, but cloth buttons are more usual.

Apprenticeship

The educated sons of wealthy merchants went into business at a very early age: in Florence, Matteo Corsini registered his son Neri at the *Mercanzia* (Guild of Merchants) when he was only seven years old.

Less wealthy men paid master craftsmen to take their sons into their homes as apprentices, to teach them their trade, which could be anything from candle-making or baking to thatching or road-mending. Girls, also, were placed as apprentices, but in such cases the master's wife would take charge of them. Most apprenticeships began when the child was between the ages of seven and nine – although one London cutler discovered that the little girl he had agreed to take was only three years old!

Apprentices were forbidden by law to marry or leave their master. Many were ill-treated; in London in 1371, for instance, Thomas and William Sewale were released

from their apprenticeship by the Court of Common Pleas because their master was in prison and his wife was not feeding them. The court found that she had beaten them cruelly and had blinded William in one eye.

After seven years the apprenticeship ended and the young man became a journeyman, travelling from town to town and working for different masters to gain experience. Historians have found few records of journey-women. After several years, a journeyman could join a guild. He paid a fee and presented a 'masterpiece' of his work to show his skill. He was then allowed to open his own shop and take on apprentices.

Above, left to right: at first the new apprentice watches the cooper shape the staves and 'raise' the barrel by fixing the staves into the bands. Heating the barrel over a brazier makes it possible to bend the staves.

Below, left to right: later, the cooper teaches the apprentice to shave the inside of the barrel, to cut the groove for the lid, and to hammer the final band into position. The barrel is put in a cradle to make the bunghole and is finally branded with the cooper's mark.

Schools

In the fourteenth century a lord's son might be educated in a monastery school, or as a page-boy in a noble household. The daughters of wealthy families sometimes attended a convent school or had a private tutor at

home. In France and Germany less wealthy children went to 'little schools', where both boys and girls were taught religion, good behaviour, singing, counting and a little Latin. Sometimes, monks set up an 'outside' school, in a building situated outside the monastery walls, for local children who did not intend to become monks or priests. Young children were taught to read by the alphabet method, learning how to put the sounds of the letters together to make the word. Their first reading book was usually a psalter, a book of the psalms of the Bible.

As towns and trade grew, however, businessmen wanted a better education for their sons. Town councils, guilds and some

merchants set money aside to buy books and employ a schoolmaster. These schools were called *stadtschulen* (state schools) in Germany, and grammar schools in England. They were for boys only. Most pupils were between the ages of about seven and fourteen, although one pupil complained that he had been beaten so badly that he had to leave school – at the age of 20! The pupils were taught all together in the same room. Work continued all day with only a lunchtime break. There was no homework or private study as most pupils did not own any books. Lessons were beaten into the boys. In Oxford, England, one teacher fell into the river and drowned while collecting branches to be used for flogging.

Although these schools did not charge fees, education was still costly. Books, paper and ink were too expensive for most pupils. A small textbook could cost 12s. (see page 63), although according to an English writer of 1345, pupils still ruined them with their greasy fingers, scribbled notes and careless behaviour: 'In winter it is chilly, his nose runs, and he does not even bother to wipe it until it has dripped and dirtied the book.'

The teacher reads from a text book written in AD 350 by Donatus, a Roman teacher, then he asks questions. Above left: a boy practises writing, using a stylus, on a wax tablet. Pupils spell words however they want, as there are no dictionaries in the Middle Ages. Older pupils learn Latin – the language used for trade negotiations with foreign merchants – and some arithmetic.

It is difficult to do sums using Roman numerals, so some schools have tally sticks (above). Most pupils are taught to calculate using their fingers or counting boards (left). However, they spend more time learning the religious significance of numbers. Three, for example, is the number for God (the Father, Son and Holy Spirit). Seven is the number for humans, because it is believed that they are made of four elements – earth, fire, air and water – and have a heart, a soul and a mind.

Betrothal

Most wealthy men married when they were over 30. A son came into his inheritance on marriage, so parents often delayed the ceremony as long as possible. Women married earlier, usually when they were about 20, but were sometimes betrothed (promised in marriage) as young as seven.

For the rich, marriage was the alliance of two families. It usually started with a business meeting to discuss the dowry (in medieval times this was a payment made by the groom to the bride's father). Representatives of the two families agreed the contract with a handshake.

Only then did the couple meet. They had little personal choice of partner, although the Italian preacher Fra Bernardino told a story of a very tall girl who refused to marry a very short man.

There was then a meeting to read the contract, followed by the 'ring day' (marriage ceremony) in the church porch. It was like a modern wedding service, except that the bride always promised to 'obey', and also to be 'bonere and buxom' (pleasant and easygoing). Finally, the wife rode to her husband's house on a white horse.

Poor people usually married at the church gate, although a promise – or even a rush ring tied around the girl's finger – was sufficient. Witnesses threw grain and sawdust over the couple to wish them a prosperous marriage. Even a poor marriage was celebrated with feasting and a riotous charivari (dance).

This girl's parents have arranged her betrothal to the son of a wealthy merchant. The agreement is drawn up by a lawyer. It is an agreement *de futura* (a promise to marry in the future) which is not binding. A contract *de praesenti* (of the present), on the other hand, needs the pope's special permission to be broken.

The Plague Arrives

'In AD 1348,' wrote the French historian Jean de Venette, 'in addition to famine and war, plague appeared in the world.'

During the 1330s, stories reached Europe of great catastrophes in the Far East – floods, famines, locusts, and a plague that killed two-thirds of the people. The disease worked its way across Asia. In 1345 it reached the Black Sea; in 1347 it arrived in Egypt. That same year a Genoese fleet docked in Sicily 'full of infected sailors, who died one after the other'.

Giovanni Villani, the chronicler of Florence, described the disease: 'There appeared certain swellings in the groin and under the armpit, the victims spat blood, and in three days they were dead.' The swellings oozed blood and pus, and were followed by spreading boils and black marks on the skin. Everything about the patient smelt foul.

The disease was terrifyingly infectious. Guy de Chauliac, the Pope's doctor, declared that you could catch the disease 'just by looking at the sick people'. A Parisian doctor, Simon de Covino, wrote that 'one sick person could infect the whole world'. He called the disease *pestis inguinaria* (plague of the groin). Later, it came to be called the Black Death, from the colour of the buboes (swellings).

By 1348 the plague had spread to Spain, France and England. The Scots, who in 1348 had mocked their old enemies the English, died by the thousand in 1349. In the same year an English wool ship, its crew all dead, drifted ashore at Bergen in Norway; the plague had reached Scandinavia.

Spreading along the trade routes, the plague is brought into town by a travelling merchant, who suddenly falls off his packhorse. The bystanders discover that he is already dead. Within a week hundreds of other people will be dead or dying.

Treating the Sick

'The doctors could give no help at all, especially as they were afraid to visit the sick,' wrote Guy de Chauliac. 'Even if they did, they earned no fees, for everyone who caught the plague died.'

Many medieval doctors thought that all disease was the result of a poisonous miasma (bad smell). To overcome it, doctors threw aromatic powders onto the fire and burnt lighted tapers. Often a doctor would hold a dried orange packed with herbs or a pomander of sweet-smelling substances over his nose. Some doctors made their patients sit in the sewers, believing that the smell of excrement would drive out the miasma. When the plague came to Avignon in the summer of 1348, de Chauliac sent the Pope away to a castle on the River Rhône, with orders to sit alone in a room between two enormous fires. It worked – the Pope survived.

Only rich people could afford a doctor.

When they became ill they were given pills and potions made from strange ingredients: cooked onions, ten-year-old treacle, herbs such as peppermint and aloes, metallic powders such as arsenic and sal ammoniac – even crushed emeralds.

Nothing worked. Some doctors were seized by the plague while tending the sick and died before their patients. Many others fled. 'As for me,' confided de Chauliac, 'to avoid disgrace I did not dare leave, but still I was in continual fear.'

A doctor examines the patient's urine. He will make a diagnosis from its colour. He consults a urine chart and his vade-mecum ('go with me'), a reference book he carries with him. The urine of a plague patient is blood red. If he thinks the patient will die, he will break the flask.

Another doctor holds a cloth soaked in vinegar over his nose while he treats the patient. Believing in the 'use of opposites', he will counteract the fever by keeping the patient cold and making him lie still. In the meantime he has lanced the buboes and dressed them with a herbal salve (ointment), and is now removing any 'bad' blood by bleeding the patient. It is important, he believes, to open certain veins, selected according to the position of the stars.

The Triumph of Death

In medieval times people believed that life on earth was unimportant compared to the eternal life, so they were usually careful to observe all the religious rituals connected with death. A dying man was given the last rites by a priest. His body, draped in black, was carried in a procession to the church. After the burial service, he was laid in as large a tomb as he could afford. Men and women were paid to pray all night for his soul: in parts of Europe this 'wake' was a wild party, where guests wore masks, got drunk and mocked the corpse.

During the Black Death, however, it was difficult to arrange a Christian funeral, because almost all the priests had either died or run away. The Italian chronicler Agnolo di Tura wrote that people were buried 'without priest or church service. Nor did the death bell sound'. In Venice, uneducated boys sang prayers for the dead which they had learned by rote. In England the Bishop of Bath and Wells declared that when there were no priests available, anyone could hear a dying person's last confession – even a woman, if a man was not present.

So many people died that it was almost impossible to bury the dead. People simply dropped dead in the streets and fields, leaving their animals to roam free. Sometimes bodies were buried so hastily that at night dogs dug them up and ate them. In Avignon corpses were thrown into the river because the cemeteries were full.

In parts of Italy 'none could be found to bury the dead for money or friendship', Agnolo di Tura wrote. 'Great pits were dug and piled deep with the multitude of dead.' In some places bodies lay rotting in the streets for many days.

The house of an infected family is boarded up. The corpses are collected at night by local criminals and poor men who, for a fee, cart them to the cemeteries. The citizens fear these men as much as the plague.

The Flagellants

Even today medical historians disagree about which disease the Black Death was, although most think it was the bubonic plague.

Medieval writers were even more mystified. The Bishop of Aarhus, in Denmark, blamed 'the four stinks of stable, fields, streets and dead flesh'. Guy de Chauliac thought the cause was 'a conjunction of Saturn, Jupiter and Mars, which had taken place in 1345'. Some people, blaming the south wind, built their houses with windows only on the north side.

Others agreed with King Magnus II of Sweden that 'God for the sins of the world has struck the world with a great punishment'. They began to live holier lives, to try to make God less angry. In France, many people stopped swearing and gambling, and manufacturers turned dice into rosary beads. Huge religious processions were held.

The flagellant movement spread all over Europe. Groups of flagellants, up to three hundred strong, passed from town to town. They marched for 33⅓ days (one for each of Christ's years on earth), scourging themselves and each other with leather whips tipped with iron spikes. In this way they hoped to obtain God's forgiveness. Sometimes the spectators cried, howled and tore their hair. They tried to catch the flagellants' blood on their handkerchiefs, believing that it had the power to work miracles.

The Pope, fearing a revolution, banned the movement in October 1349. Many flagellants were arrested and put to death.

The flagellants have promised to obey their leader and are not allowed to wash, shave or change their clothes. At each town they put on displays two or three times a day, whipping themselves and each other until their blood flows. The men are beaten if they even speak to a woman. If a priest joins the group, they must start all over again.

Results of the Plague

In Ireland, Brother John Clyn, the last surviving monk in his monastery, thought that the whole world was 'in the grasp of the Evil One'. He feared that all mankind would die.

In Florence, the historian Giovanni Villani was more hopeful. 'The plague lasted till…', he wrote, leaving a space to continue the sentence – but he did not live to fill in the date.

Medieval writers, overwhelmed by the shock of the plague, exaggerated its effect. A French chronicler claimed that in Marseilles fifty thousand people died – more than the entire population of the town. In England,

Bishop Edyndon of Winchester wrote in biblical tones of countries 'deprived of their children, stripped of their populations; abodes of horror, deserts of barrenness'.

In all, perhaps a third of the population of Europe died. In towns the death rate seems to have been much higher. In Venice it was 60 per cent. In Avignon eleven thousand corpses were buried in six weeks. In some places all the inhabitants died or ran away. When the Bishop of Durham called his tenants together in 1380, no one came from the village of West Boldon 'because they are all dead'.

Eventually the Black Death left Europe and moved on into Russia. In 1350 Pope Clement VI announced a jubilee year. A million pilgrims made their way to Rome to celebrate the survival of humanity. The Black Death, however, was just the beginning. Plague returned in 1360, again in 1369, and then every four to twelve years until the sixteenth century.

Reactions

The emotional pain of the plague was almost unbearable. 'My sons Amerigo and Martino died on the same day, in my arms,' wrote Lapo Mazzei, an Italian merchant. 'And my daughter Antonia in bed, sick to death, and the middle boy with her. How my heart was broken.'

People reacted in different ways. In Austria,

'men walked about as if mad'. In Florence the poor 'became idle and unwilling to work'. According to the poet Boccaccio, 'some people decided that wild living would keep them alive. They spent all their time drinking and revelling in tavern after tavern'. Exaggerated fashions became popular; both sexes wore tight jackets with slashed sleeves and large hoods, and 'looked more like devils than ordinary people'.

The poor took over the houses of rich families who had died, and behaved riotously. Anyone who developed a boil was immediately deserted. Parents even abandoned their children.

Many people looked for a scapegoat, claiming that the plague had occurred because the wells had been poisoned. The Spanish blamed the Arabs, the French blamed the English, everybody blamed the lepers. Anybody found with a suspicious powder was made to swallow it. Finally, in 1348, in Neustadt in Germany, a Jewish doctor confessed under torture that a rabbi had given him powders to poison the wells. Led by the flagellants, and supported by everybody who was in debt to the Jewish moneylenders, pogroms (organized killings) took place all over Europe, particularly in Germany. In Hamburg, the Jews' houses were bricked up and the families inside were left to starve. In Speyer the Jews were forced to climb into wine casks, which were then nailed up and thrown in the river. The citizens of Basle locked the Jews in a wooden building on an island in the river and burned them to death.

The Black Death causes deep despair amongst the people of western Europe, who become obsessed with death and decay.

Far left: a fourteenth-century stained-glass window in an English church shows death claiming a bishop.

Above left: the tomb of the French nobleman François de Sarra, who died in 1360. Toads are eating his face and worms slide over his arms.

Below: in the fourteenth century a processional play called the *Danse Macabre* becomes common in many parts of Europe. These artists are painting a fresco in which men dressed as skeletons perform a dance of death with figures representing all levels of society, including a pope, an emperor, a bishop, a merchant, lords, ladies, a monk and a peasant. An inscription will be added to warn the onlooker: 'This is you'.

War and the Town

There were some things that the Black Death did not change. In particular, the Hundred Years War between England and France continued as though nothing had happened.

In the fourteenth century war was thought to be honourable and Christian. Many men – such as Bascot de Mauleon, whom the French chronicler Jean Froissart met in 1388 – spent their whole lives travelling from one war to the next, seeking 'better fighting'. War was a man's job, although in Italy in 1343 the scholar Petrarch wrote that he had met 'a mighty woman' called Maria, who cared 'not for charms, but for arms'.

After the battles of Crécy (1346) and Poitiers (1356) – when the French cavalry were slaughtered – military commanders tried to avoid pitched battles. Instead, they raided the countryside, burning the crops in an attempt to cause famine. These destructive raids were called *chevauchées*.

Sometimes an army would besiege a town. The local militia (soldiers) defended the walls as well as they could, firing arrows and throwing large stones at the attackers. They would make surprise attacks on the besiegers, doing as much damage as possible before the enemy had a chance to fight back. As food supplies ran short, however, the townspeople were reduced to eating dogs, cats and even rats. Bored and frustrated, a besieging army often massacred the entire population of a town after a long siege. When Limoges was captured in 1370, only the three French knights who had led the defence were spared, along with the Bishop of Limoges, who was freed at the Pope's request. The English soldiers dragged out the rest of the three thousand citizens and slit their throats, despite their pleas for mercy.

In 1373, during a *chevauchée* lasting six months, the English invaders are followed by the French army. The two sides are so close that the soldiers can swap jokes. Although the English are destroying the countryside and slaughtering the peasants, the two French knights (on horses, centre) refuse to risk starting a battle.

Mercenaries

During the lulls between the campaigns of the Hundred Years War, the armies were disbanded and towns found themselves at the mercy of large bands of unemployed soldiers which were left wandering the countryside.

These groups were called Free Companies because they were mercenaries: they were prepared to fight for any government or city that would pay them. Sometimes they could be bribed to go away – a company led by the French knight Bertrand du Guesclin was given a blessing and 200,000 francs (see page 63) when it passed through Avignon. The Pope remarked ruefully that people normally paid him for a blessing.

At other times the mercenaries lived by plunder. Bascot de Mauleon (see page 46) claimed that he had made a fortune from 'robbery, protection money and strokes of

48

luck'. Du Guesclin admitted that he had 'attacked women, burned houses, killed children, taken men ransom, eaten their animals and drunk their wine'. The people of one village threw themselves into the river when they heard that the English knight Sir Richard Knollys was coming. 'When we rode out, the country trembled before us,' another company leader boasted.

The knights and nobles who led the Free Companies were rewarded by governments and accepted into wealthy society. After years of killing, Eustace d'Aubrecicourt married a niece of the Queen of England. Some people did complain, however. The French writer Jean de Venette criticized the knights and the government for not defending the country against the marauders.

The Church teaches that the knights protect the people. The householders, whose food and possessions are being stolen, know that this is not true.

The Excesses of the Rich

In the Middle Ages people loved feasting and the 'delight of meats'. This was especially true after the Black Death, when the rich decided to enjoy life while they could and 'abandoned themselves to the sin of gluttony'

Their feasts were extravagant displays of wealth and plenty. When the Holy Roman Emperor visited the Count of Savoy in 1365, the guests were served by mounted knights, who carried the food on plates attached to the points of their lances.

In 1368 the marriage feast of Violante Visconti, daughter of the Duke of Milan, comprised 30 courses of meat and fish, including suckling pigs with crabs, hare with pike, and calf with trout. All the meat and fish was gilded – covered with a paste made from egg yolks, saffron, flour and gold leaf. The left-over food alone fed a thousand servants. In

between each course gifts of armour, falcons, horses, war-dogs and fat oxen were exchanged.

Hosts tried to surprise their guests with sensational gimmicks. At a banquet in France the ceiling opened and the food was lowered on machines disguised to look like clouds. The final course was accompanied by a shower of scented water and sweetmeats (sweet cakes).

In 1399, Richard II of England entertained on a massive scale. For each of the 12 days of Christmas his cooks killed 28 oxen and 300 sheep, as well as 'fowl without number', to feed ten thousand guests.

Sitting on benches (the word banquet comes from the French word *banc*, meaning bench) guests eat with knife, spoon and fingers only. They use their little finger to take the rich sauces from the bowls on the table. As they do not have dinner plates, the food will be served on thick slices of bread which will later be given to the poor. The floor has been scattered with sweet-smelling flowers and fragrant herbs.

The Suffering of the Poor

The Black Death, combined with the destruction caused by the Hundred Years War and the bad weather, seriously damaged the economy of western Europe. Many towns declined, particularly in Italy. Trade had almost ceased during the plague; now it clogged up with lawsuits because so many lawyers had died. There were not enough labourers to cultivate the land. Shortages led to higher prices. The crime rate increased. The population continued to fall.

Old people, who had to rely on others to look after them, suffered most. The elderly usually handed over ownership of their business and home to a son or neighbour, and moved into a room in the house (sometimes called the western chamber) to be looked after by the family. However, the son and daughter-in-law, who had the 'labour of waschyng and wryngyng and the costage in fyryng', were often tempted to neglect their ageing relatives. Inquests held in the fourteenth century showed that many old people were left to look after themselves. One old lady fell into a well trying to fetch water; another drowned in a stream when she left her son's house to beg for bread in a nearby town.

The Merchant's Tale, written in 1387 by the English writer Chaucer, is about an old man whose young wife took a lover. It shows the careless, mocking attitude that some young people took towards the old.

This old man's children died in the plague. Now he lives alone in poverty in his one-roomed hut, on a diet of vegetable stew, pease pudding (boiled dried peas) and beanflour bread. Like many poor people, he keeps a pig, which shares his cottage and his food.

Above: the walls of many peasants' huts are made of wattle and daub – interwoven sticks daubed with a mixture of clay, horse dung and straw to keep out the worst of the weather. Top: a flint house lived in by a moderately well-off peasant.

Universities

So many learned men had died during the Black Death that a number of universities and colleges were founded to 'repair the ravages of the plague'. The most famous

were the University of Prague (1348) and New College, Oxford (1379).

Conditions were harsh. At French and Scottish universities the students had to suffer the *bejan* (initiation ceremony) in which they were bullied and washed in public. They were forbidden to have fires in their rooms; yet at Padua University the windows were made of linen, and there were no glass window-panes at Prague University until 1463.

Although scholars were mostly clerics preparing for a career in the Church, they were as violent and undisciplined as the rest of society. In Oxford, students became highwaymen; in Paris they took women into the lecture halls at night. University rules forbade students to knife an examiner who asked a

difficult question – which gives some idea of how students behaved. Often there was undeclared war between town and gown (the townspeople and the university). In 1355 a mob of local people invaded Oxford University and assaulted, killed or scalped a number of students.

Universities were not places where new ideas were developed. Any lecturer who spoke against the Church's teaching had to publicly admit his error and promise to 'hold to the Catholic faith'.

Undergraduates, who are usually aged between 12 and 18, live and are taught in groups of about a dozen in halls (houses let to a teacher). A degree course lasts six years. Students study the *trivium* (grammar, rhetoric and logic) and the *quadrivium* (arithmetic, geometry, astronomy and music), along with medicine and law. Colleges (main picture) are only for postgraduates.

Below: many lecturers merely read from a book. Some students follow the text in their own books, while others chatter or sleep. Above left: precious, handwritten books are often kept safely chained in a chest.

Rebellions

During the plague the workers had realized that a shortage of labourers increased their bargaining power. In June 1349, as the Black Death raged in the French town of Amiens, the tanners had demanded higher wages 'to the great hurt of the people'. Faced with rising prices, however, the wealthy needed more money to maintain their standard of living. Governments passed laws forbidding workers to take higher wages, to wear fine clothes or to eat too well.

Writers noted that the labourers were 'filled with a spirit of rebellion'. In 1358 France suffered a peasant rebellion called the *Jacquerie* (after the padded jackets worn by the peasants in battle). Some castles were burned and a few nobles were killed.

Froissart, however, recorded that there were one hundred thousand rebels, and that 'never did men commit such vile deeds: I could never bring myself to write down what they did to the ladies'. His exaggeration shows his belief that the rebels were 'evil-doers', undermining a social order ordained by God.

In 1381 the weavers of Ghent rebelled against the Count of Flanders. In England a 'mad multitude' of twenty thousand peasants, led by an old soldier called Wat Tyler, marched on London demanding that 'lords be no more masters than ourselves'. In France, the *Maillotins* (named after the three thousand police mallets they seized) murdered the Jews and wealthy people of Paris and Rouen.

All the rebellions were eventually put down – the peasants were no match for mounted knights. 'God by His grace provided a remedy,' wrote Froissart. 'The nobles wiped them out wherever they found them, without mercy or pity.'

In Florence, crying 'Long live the people!', the *Ciompi* (lowest class) seize control of the city for a short time in 1378. They demand the right to join the guilds and the freedom to form trade unions.

The Lollard Movement

After the Black Death, many priests were accused of deserting their flocks and fleeing from the plague – somewhat unfairly, for half the clergy had died. People felt the Church had let them down; it was said that priests were only interested in the wealthier parishes and higher wages.

John Wyclif, a teacher at Oxford University in England, claimed that the priests had become too wealthy and that people should stop paying tithes (taxes) to the Church. He argued that priests were not necessary for salvation, and denied transubstantiation (the belief that the bread and wine change into the actual body and blood of Christ during the Mass). He had the Bible translated from Latin into English, so that ordinary people could understand it.

Wyclif's supporters, called Lollards, came from all levels of society. His influence spread across Europe, particularly to Bohemia. His followers, dressed in rough, homespun coats, went into the countryside, preaching their new ideas to the people and reading them the Bible in their own language. Many were even more extreme than Wyclif. Sybil Godsell said that women ought to be allowed to become priests. Another woman, Hawise Moone, wanted to give the wealth of the Church to the poor. Some Lollards claimed that Christ had taught that war was evil, so they refused to fight in the army.

The Lollards were accused of being heretics. A number of Wyclif's supporters, including John Huss in Bohemia and Jerome of Prague, were burned at the stake. The Lollards continued to meet in secret; a century later many people in northern Europe accepted their ideas in the period of religious changes called the Reformation.

This Lollard refuses to accept the doctrine of transubstantiation. He will be burned to death.

Death and Rebirth

The modern historian Barbara Tuchman has described the fourteenth century as 'a succession of wayward dangers' – a time when humanity seemed at the mercy of famine, animal murrain, plague, war, the Free Companies, rebellion and heresy.

Slowly, however, medieval Europe began to change. The Black Death was only a temporary setback; the population eventually regained its previous level. Nobles who spent extravagantly on fashionable clothes and feasting enriched the tradesmen. Money was lavished on cathedrals and colleges, which led to developments in architecture, painting and sculpture. Even war had its advantages – the Italian merchant Rinaldo degli Albizzi realized that in time of war 'the city is always full of soldiers, who must buy all their needs; tradesmen grow prosperous'.

As commerce developed, European rulers began to seek new trade routes and markets – a process which eventually led, in 1492, to Columbus's discovery of the New World.

Books brought to western Europe from the Muslim East expanded knowledge, especially of mathematics and geography. After the Black Death, doctors began to write books based on their professional experience (rather than simply accepting the opinions of ancient Greek writers) and medical knowledge began to increase. The Lollards and the peasant revolts of the fourteenth century were the first signs of Protestantism and democracy (government by the people).

The world did not end in the fourteenth century as many people had predicted. In the fifteenth and sixteenth centuries, during the periods known as the Renaissance (rebirth) and the Reformation (of the Roman Catholic Church), there were major changes in art, politics and religion, which marked the beginning of a new age.

Despite the wars, plagues and famines of the fourteenth century, life goes on. Here, nobles, traders, peasants and beggars wait for the town gates to open. Although medieval towns are small, they are vitally important centres of trade, government, religion, learning and new ideas.

How Do We Know?

In the fourteenth century, in addition to government documents and the writings of clerics, ordinary people began to keep records. Many documents have survived, such as records of court cases, guild regulations, rent rolls, cookery books, letters and poems. People began to write in their own language instead of in Latin; from the fourteenth century, for instance, comes the earliest example of a letter written by a woman in the English language.

Documents dating from the Middle Ages are difficult to read. In some cases the ink has faded completely. Where it is still visible, it is usually illegible. Medieval handwriting was often a badly formed scrawl, and people spelled words however they liked. Not only historians have had problems with this. Doing his household accounts in 1315, Lord Lancaster (see page 16) had to write off £242 'for things bought, whereof cannot be read in my note'.

It was common practice to rub out the writing on an old document and reuse the parchment. The poet Boccaccio, visiting the famous library at Monte Cassino in Italy before the Black Death, found the monks erasing priceless manuscripts so that they could copy out reading books to sell to local schoolchildren. A manuscript on which two or more texts have been written is called a palimpsest.

Nevertheless, some beautiful books have survived from the fourteenth century – for instance, the Luttrell Psalter and the *Très Riches Heures* of the Duc de Berry. The Luttrell Psalter is full of detailed drawings of country people. The *Très Riches Heures*, a book of prayers, contains scenes of country life. Monks illuminated Bible stories as if they took place in their own time. They drew the characters in medieval clothes, set against medieval backgrounds. This is useful for

the historian, who can see how people lived in medieval times.

Fact and Fiction

Many chronicles (histories) have survived from the fourteenth century. The best is Jean Froissart's account of the Hundred Years War between France and England. Froissart gathered his information himself – for instance, he interviewed Bascot de Mauleon (see page 46). Yet his witnesses almost certainly exaggerated, and Froissart then tried to make the characters even more glamorous; he admitted that he wrote 'so that men should be inspired to follow such examples'. Froissart, a Frenchman, was biased in favour of the French, and he never criticized 'the most noble Count of Blois', who was his employer.

The Christian attitudes of the writers were also reflected in the chronicles of the time. Medieval writers were greatly influenced by the Bible, which they believed was the word of God. When they described disasters or corruption, therefore, they automatically echoed the ideas and the language of the Bible (for example, see Bishop Edyndon's description of the plague on page 44).

Descriptions of military brutality all tend to be the same. In *The Flowers of History*, for example, Matthew of Westminster described an enemy soldier as 'more hardened in cruelty than Herod'. He was actually referring to the Scottish leader William Wallace, but it could have been any soldier in any army – such descriptions are standard, even down to the details of what he did, such as killing children and setting fire to churches.

The historian has to decide whether or not these stories are true. The writer might have put them in as a standard formula for military atrocities (see page 49).

Historians can also read the poems and stories written in the fourteenth century, such as Boccaccio's *Decameron*, and *The Canterbury Tales* by the English poet Geoffrey Chaucer. Both Boccaccio and Chaucer included realistic descriptions of typical characters – useful to a historian who wishes to know how people behaved in everyday life. In addition, Boccaccio and Chaucer describe what these people were thinking. The rude stories in the *Decameron* show the despair and worldliness of the years just after the plague. In Chaucer's tales we see the hatred of the clergy.

Myths and Issues

Using these sources, the historian tries to work out what life was really like. This can be difficult. For instance, did medieval people keep themselves clean? Contemporary writers complained of the foul smell of the peasants, and the 'beer, grease, bones and excrement' on the floors of houses. Basing their arguments on such sources, many historians have said that medieval families lived in total squalor. Yet we know that towns had bathhouses (see page 14) and that wealthy people tried to make rooms smell pleasant (see page 51).

What is the historian to believe? Do the frequent complaints about the dirt in the streets (see page 13) show that medieval people lived in filthy conditions? Or do they show that they objected to the rubbish and were taking steps to make their towns clean?

Words from the Past

Dom Ramon Muntaner, a Spanish soldier, was made homeless when his native town of Perelada was besieged and burned down by the French. In 1325, when he was 60, he sat down to write his memoirs. He wrote: 'I would gladly avoid the task of this story; yet it is my bounden duty to tell it, so that everybody will learn how the grace of God is the best help in danger.' It is exciting to think that you are reading the exact words and thoughts of someone who lived more than six hundred years ago. Did Dom Ramon, perhaps, pause to wonder if anyone would be reading his words hundreds of years later? If he did, he was thinking of *you*. Across the centuries, your minds can meet: you are thinking of him, and he is speaking to you.

A Note about Money

It is almost impossible to estimate what money was worth in the Middle Ages. In England there were 12 pennies (12d.) in a shilling, and 20 shillings (20s.) to the pound (£1). The French franc was roughly the equivalent of the English pound. Many people, however, did not use money at all. They bartered, exchanging goods for other goods.

All prices, moreover, need to be considered in relation to the incomes of the people of the time – a labourer's daily wage was 4d., a knight's daily wage in battle was 2s., while the income of a very rich lord might be £8,000 a year.

Prices changed all the time, and it is difficult to make comparisons because the relative prices of goods were so different. For example, in the Middle Ages, 240 sheets of parchment cost 10s. – almost as much as a cow.

Opposite page: a picture from the Luttrell Psalter, *c.* 1340, showing Sir Geoffrey Luttrell with his wife and daughter-in-law.

Index

OTHER IMPORTANT EVENTS

● Marco Polo visits China (1271)

THE HUNDRED YEARS W

Fall of Acre:
end of the Crusades
(1291)

Philip IV, King of France (1285 - 1314)

Froissart, French chronicler (

Pope Boniface VIII (1294 - 1303)

Boccaccio wri

Petrarch, Italian poet laureate (1304 - 1374)

Chaucer, English write

1280	1290	1300	1310	1320	1330	1340	

Dom Ramon Muntaner
writes his memoirs (page 63)

Great Famine in Europe (page 9)

EVENTS MENTIONED
IN THIS BOOK

The

Battle of

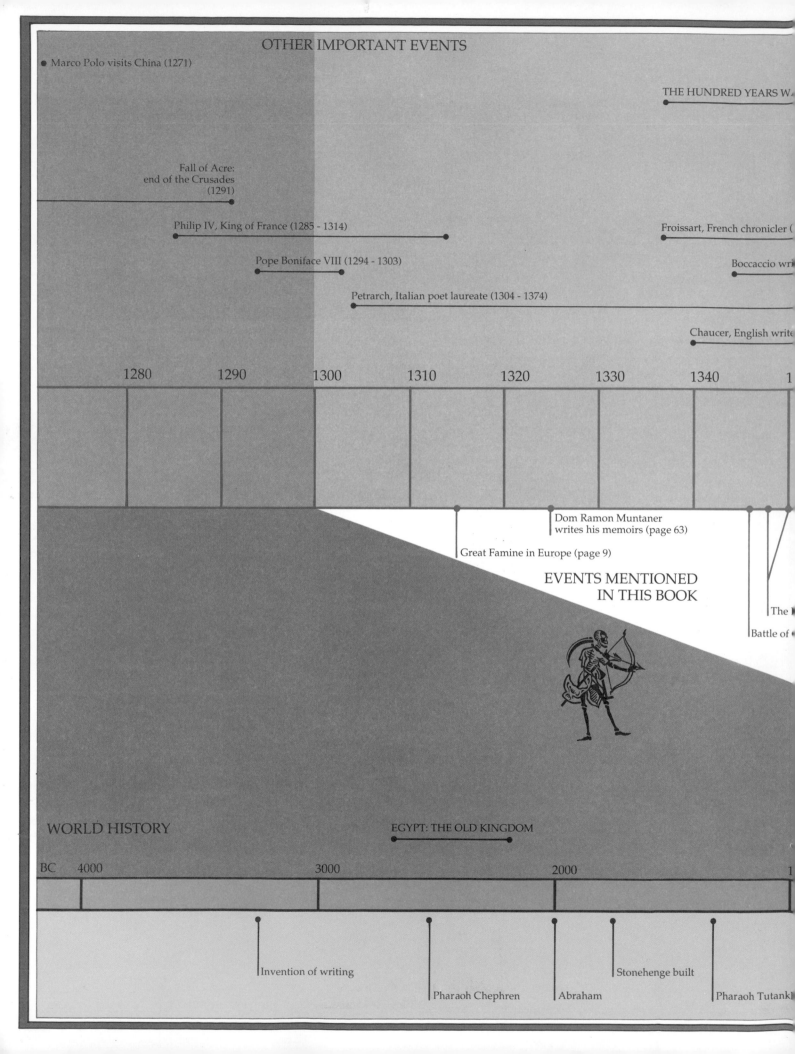

WORLD HISTORY

EGYPT: THE OLD KINGDOM

BC	4000		3000		2000		1

Invention of writing

Stonehenge built

Pharaoh Chephren

Abraham

Pharaoh Tutankl